GREEN GOLD

ECO-SOLUTIONS FOR A
RICHER ECO-NOMY

by *melvia miller*

GREEN GOLD

ECO-SOLUTIONS FOR A RICHER **ECO-NOMY**

SPECIAL EDITION

Published by **Edutainment Enterprises**

EMAIL = **eco.farmacy@gmail.com**

Printed in the U.S.A.

This book belongs to: _____

Phone = ___(_____)_____

All praise and thanks to the Great Spirit for blessing me with the talent, skills, and education to compose this book.

DEDICATION:

This book is dedicated to my 2 wonderful sons, Malik and Mikal, who have been the light and delight of my life. My sons are very special people and will receive most of the benefits, proceeds and honors derived from the sales of my books. I could not have accomplished the completion of this book without my 2 sons.

THANKS:

A SPECIAL THANKS TO MY MOTHER AND FATHER for raising me. I could not have accomplished this writing project without the help, support and love of all of my many friends. I deeply appreciate all of the people who have assisted me in various ways throughout my life.

~Melvia F. Miller *(aka: "the Soulful Dr. Seuss)*

############

DISCLAIMER: The information, resources and websites in this book have been compiled to assist you in your research. The author of this book makes no promises, claims or guarantees that you will get rich from reading this book. We only promise that your awareness of how to do it will be greatly increased. It is up to you to check out each of these sources and companies to find out if what they offer will suit your needs and desires.
HAVE A MILLION DOLLAR DAY!

Did you know?

262 million people were affected
by climate disasters in 2004,
more than 98 per cent of them
in developing countries

TABLE OF CONTENTS:

Page:

INTRODUCTION -------------------- 7

WHY GO GREEN ? ----------------- 17

*****NATURE'S GIFTS** --------------- 21

CHAPTER ONE ------------------------- 29
CLIMATE INFO.... CARTOONS

CHAPTER TWO ------------------------ 39

ECO-FRIENDLY BUSINESS
BEGIN AT HOME
   *Natural cleaners & pesticides
START A BUSINESS
BOOST YOUR INCOME
MAIL ORDER 101

CHAPTER THREE ---------------------- 67
GO BIG IN A GREEN BIZ
HELP STOP HUNGER

BUSINESS PLANS -------------------- 77
* BUSINESS STRUCTURES
* BUSINESS PLANS

TIPS FOR SURVIVING WEATHER DISASTERS ----- 80

EDUTAINMENT ACTIVITIES ---------- 85

ABOUT THE AUTHOR -------------------- 90

Global warming

Everyone's problem

THE DAY AFTER TOMORROW

THE MOVIE IS FICTIONAL
CLIMATE CHANGE IS REAL

EARN WHILE YOU LEARN !

Help Save the Planet

PROSPER from the *"words of wisdom"*
from Super Sistah !
www.success-secrets.ws

Introduction

Today we live in an uncertain future when we try to project where humanity will be just one hundred years from now. The environment we all live in is rapidly being consumed and wasted so that short term gains can be made just for individuals.

Remember that all living things are **connected**, therefore, care for your environment as you would yourself. There are many things we can all do to live more in harmony with the environment. Simple things like recycling, planting trees, using "eco-friendly household products, installing solar panels, using non-polluting electric or bio-diesel powered cars, and responsible consumer practices can make a big difference. Returning to a natural and more simple lifestyle is not a step backwards in time but rather, one leap forward into a future lifestyle that supports all, for when something is working in harmony with the Earth -- all must benefit.

HOPI INDIAN PREDICTIONS:

*"Those who return to the ways given to us in the original teachings, and live a natural way of life will not be touched by the coming of the **Purifier**. They will survive and build the new world. Only in the ancient teachings will the ability to understand the messages be found."*

What has gone wrong ?

"Only when the last tree has died and the last river been poisoned and the last fish been caught will we realize we cannot eat money." ~ Cree Indian Proverb

The weather is one of the biggest news items on TV and radio every day....and the SCARIEST !

SHAKE, RATTLE, ROLL, AND BLOW -- Monster tornadoes have repeatedly devastated the midwest U.S.A.-- (Oklahoma, Colorado, Texas, Tennessee, Iowa, etc.) destroying thousands of buildings & homes, and killing people. Winds ripped the roofs off buildings and tossed cars and trucks around like they were toys. Flooding has affected coastal towns.... causing millions of dollars in damages.

The POLAR CAPS are melting, and wild fires have burned large areas because of the drought-dried landscape in various areas of the country. Flooding is affecting many cities, while wildfires burn.

Many people have become 'divorced' from Nature... and some are *"anti-nature"*... in their actions and policies.

The wild weather -- monster typhoons, floods, blizzards, typhoons, hurricanes, earthquakes ...and the melting polar ice caps are results of the WARMING PLANET.

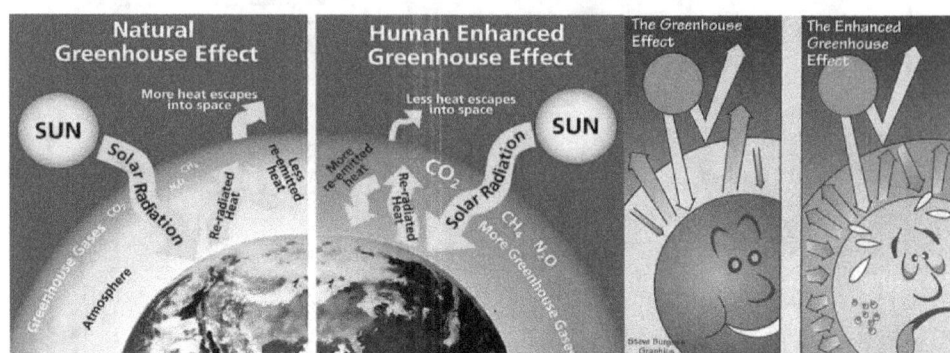

The **GREEN HOUSE EFFECT** lies at the root of **CLIMATE CHANGE** – due to the waste, pollution, and CO2, methane, and other gases trapping heat. And there are other problems --*such as*: destruction of Rainforests, factory smoke & toxic emissions & dropping bombs -- which contribute to imbalancing the **ECO-SYSTEM.**

What price do we pay to live in the world as it is currently set up ?

- We eat food that is killing us, consume all manner of chemicals that we don't even know about, work in jobs we hate to buy items we more than likely don't need in the first place. We work in factories that blow poison fumes into the air. We drive vehicles that spew toxic emissions into our air that makes us sick. We waste lots of money buying too much junk into our homes... and with many of these items being made at the expense of the death of our most valuable resource, the Earth. We dump all sorts of chemicals into our rivers lakes and oceans – which kill the fish and harm the coral reef. Living like zombie robots, we often don't even know our neighbors -- let alone work with them in any form of extended community.

Forests are the world's air-conditioning system— the lungs of the planet.
— and we are on the verge of switching it off.

Prince Charles

MARVIN GAYE
MERCY, MERCY ME

Words from the classic 'ECOLOGY' song by Marvin Gaye

"Mercy, Mercy Me (The Ecology)"

Woo ah, mercy mercy me....Ah things ain't what they used to be, no no....
Where did all the blue skies go?
Poison is the wind that blows from the north and south and east....Woo mercy, mercy me, mercy ...
Ah things ain't what they used to be, no no...
Oil wasted on the ocean and upon our seas, fish full of mercury....Ah oh mercy, mercy me --
Ah things ain't what they used to be, no no....
Radiation under ground and in the sky --
Animals and birds who live nearby are dying...

Edutainment Enterprises
Now available = books, games, DVDs, health products ...& more !

www.authorsden.com/melviafmiller

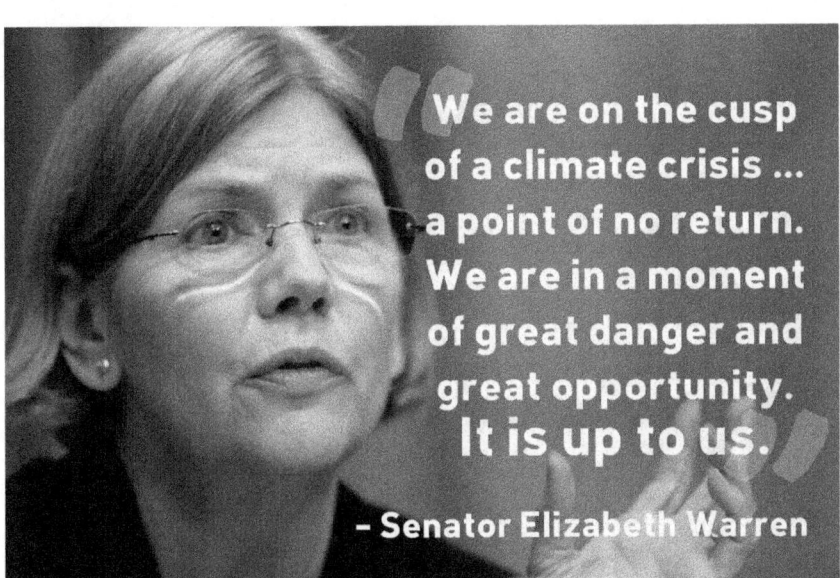

"We are on the cusp of a climate crisis ... a point of no return. We are in a moment of great danger and great opportunity. It is up to us."

– Senator Elizabeth Warren

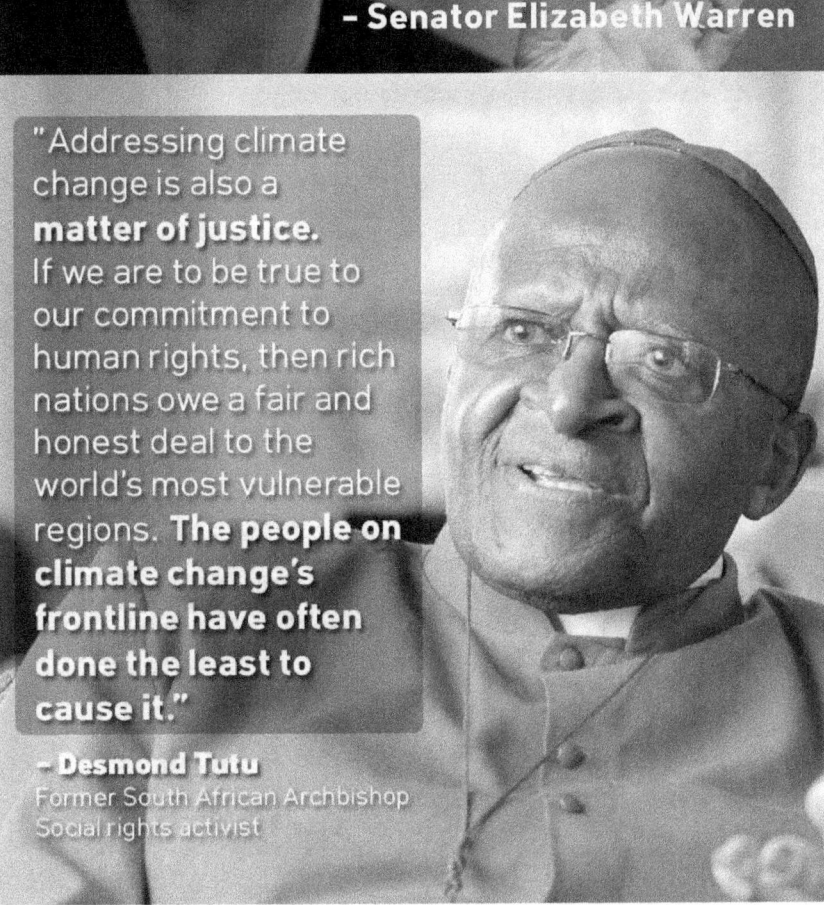

"Addressing climate change is also a **matter of justice.** If we are to be true to our commitment to human rights, then rich nations owe a fair and honest deal to the world's most vulnerable regions. **The people on climate change's frontline have often done the least to cause it.**"

– Desmond Tutu
Former South African Archbishop
Social rights activist

According to Al Gore -- 'Watching TV News *on Extreme Weather is like a Nature Hike through the Book of Revelation'*--

"We the human species are confronting a planetary emergency--a threat to the survival of our civilization that is gathering ominous and destructive potential... the earth has a fever. And the fever is rising...Indeed, without realizing it, we have begun to wage war on earth itself..." --Al Gore, Nobel Prize acceptance speech, 2007

Al Gore has issued scientific explanations for our climate problems.

He is not the only or the first to warn us about mistreating the environment.

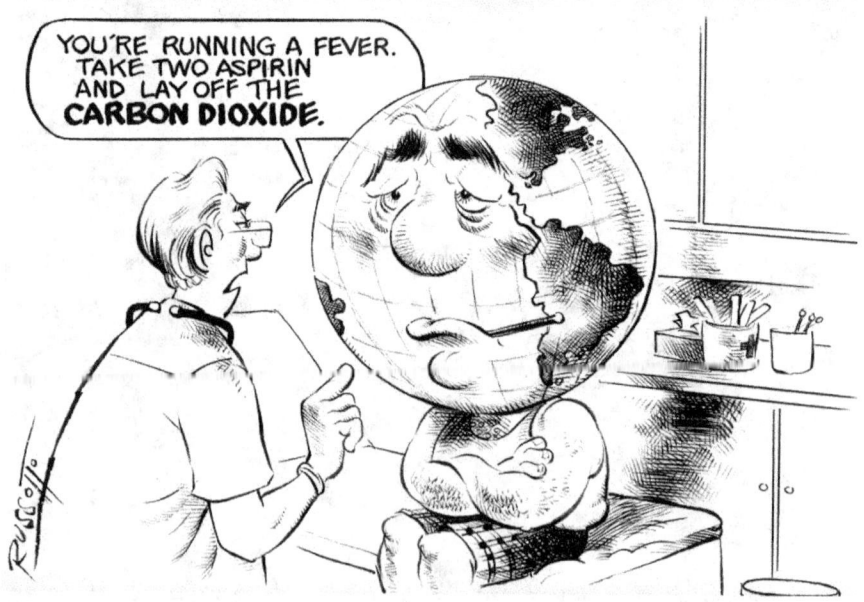

GREEN GOLD

In addition, air pollution *(exhaust fumes, killing the rainforests, smoke, pesticides, etc.)* have caused our normal oxygen content of the atmosphere to be reduced from 40% to only 20%. Air pollution and water pollution are major causes of diseased bodies.

Deforestation is taking place in areas such as — destruction, burning of and cutting down **RAINFORESTS**...via logging for lumber, pulpwood, paper products, and fuel wood. By cutting down the **RAINFORESTS** and other plants, they have reduced all buffers against environmental imbalances.

These problems influence and effect society in many ways --

-ECONOMIC.... AGRICULTURE.... JOBS..... HEALTH....

INFRASTRUCTURE DAMAGE..... HOUSING.... etc.

Wild weather has effect most parts of the world, including the U.S.A. – and is causing huge problems for the economy and health --

WHY IS THIS HAPPENING ?

Scientists & researchers believe that most is caused by...

" THE GREENHOUSE EFFECT "--

....which is an increase in concentration of the main **greenhouse gases**

* carbon dioxide,
* methane,
* nitrous oxide, and
* fluorocarbons.... (and other pollutants)

Fossil Fuels are created chiefly by the decay of plants from millions of years ago. Companies have found ways to use it as energy: *coal, oil and natural gas* to generate power -- which we have used to heat our homes, power our factories, and run our cars, etc. These fossil fuels contain carbon, and when they are burned, they combine with oxygen, forming carbon dioxide. But simultaneously, burning fossil fuels is contributing to the pollution that is killing us all.

The *Green Gold Strategy* offers the opportunity for economic and environmental revitalization by favoring renewable, sustainable approaches to ECONOMIC DEVELOPMENT-- *such as:* clean energy, non-polluting fuels, recycling waste, degradable plastic products, natural health products, and similar services that improve our health, lifestyles... and protect the environment.

You quite literally have the ability to mold various areas of your life, based on how you choose to think, believe and feel!! That is how our world was created to operate.   We can improve our conditions by learning to the ways of NATURE and sharing the wealth.

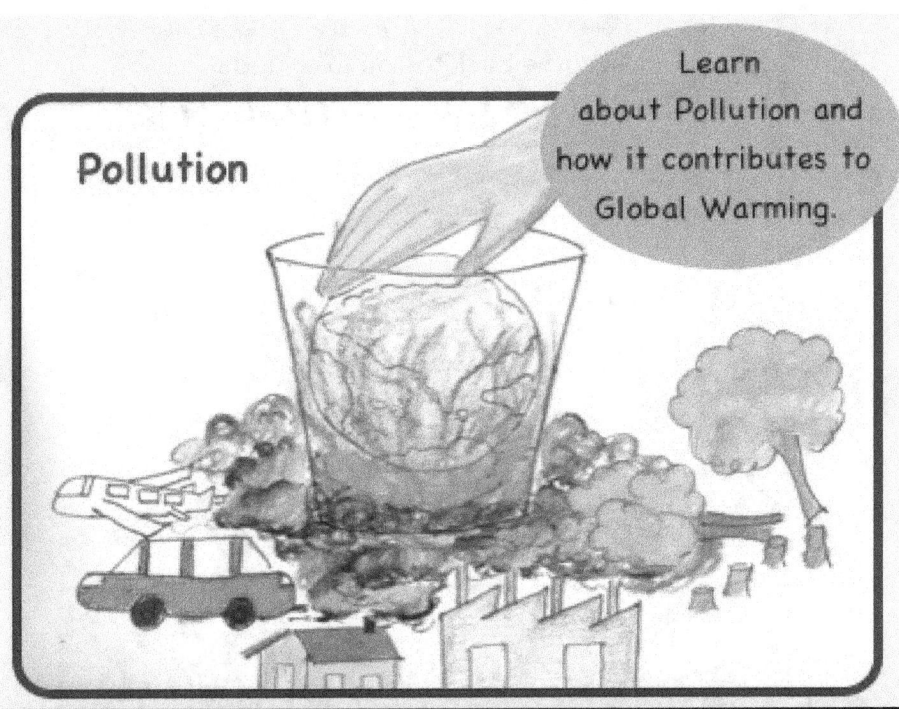

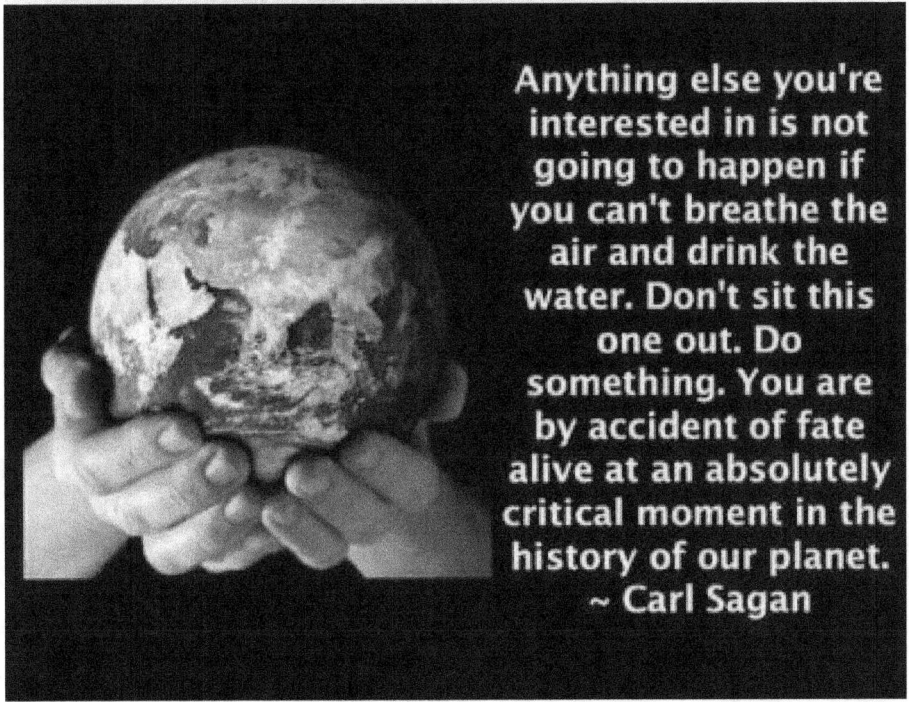

"Plant seeds of *happiness, hope, success,* and *love;*
it will all come back to you in abundance.
This is the law of *nature."*

- Steve Maraboli, Life, the Truth, and Being Free

Natural News.com

The world we are experiencing today is the
result of our collective consciousness,
and if we want a new world, each of us must
start taking responsibility for helping create it.

~Rosemary Fillmore Rhea~

EmilysQuotes.Com

Take care of the Earth
AND SHE WILL TAKE CARE OF YOU

Listen to the
voice of nature,
For it holds
treasures for you.

-Huron-

EmilysQuotes.Com

NATURE OFFERS MANY GIFTS

Through the synergy of various elements-- including minerals and gases--- *(hydrogen, oxygen, carbon, phosphorous, sulfur, etc.)* -- the necessities for life came into being. Water exists on this planet and is essential for life on Earth. Without water, this planet would be nothing more than a big rock floating through space. Air is also essential for life. Light is provided by our sun, which is a huge ball of nuclear fission fire.

Soil, air, fire, and water are the basic elements present in an **well-balanced eco-system** that sustains life and makes Earth the beautiful place that it is. Fire, water, metal, wood, air, and earth (soil) are recognized as the basic ingredients of all material things.

Plants absorb sunlight and, with that energy, chlorophyll changes water and carbon dioxide absorbed from the air into sugar. This natural process – called: **PHOTOSYNTHESIS** releases oxygen, water, and carbohydrates as by-products.

Modern research studies have shown that there is more to **GREEN** than just myths and old superstitions. And three recent studies have found that living near such areas has beneficial effects on our health and the health of our children.

" Nature is the broadcasting station
for the highest power. "

~ Dr. George Washington Carver (Agricultural Botanist, scientist)

Let Nature be your guide!

Love • Self-Control • Goodness • Joy • Gentleness • Kindness • Patience • Peace • Faithfulness

CO2 emissions

algae

algae farms

CO2 escaping into the atmosphere is captured and fed to algae

algae doubles its' size every 24 hours

farms produce oil, ethanol and many other products

HEMP FOR FUEL

Hemp makes more fuel, fiber food & medicine than any other plant, and it was the first crop sown, over 12,000 years ago. An acre of hemp produces 300 gallons of oil, 3 tons of protein, and 30 tons of fiber a year.

www.hemp.org

Answers to most of our problems are right before our eyes:
NATURE PROVIDES EVERYTHING WE NEED...

Bees make honey ---

Cows produce milk....

Eggs come from chickens...

"Nature provides enough for everyone's needs,
but not for every man's greed." ~ Confuscius

THERE ARE SOLUTIONS TO THESE PROBLEMS...

Learn from the examples set by others who have done it.

George Washington Carver's Products

Carver helped farmers by developing new uses for peanuts, sweet potatoes, and soybeans. It became economically viable to produce these crops because there were more uses for them, and in turn, greater demand. This helped the economy of the South evolve from a cotton monoculture.

Carver is best known for his work with peanuts. He developed over 300 uses for peanuts, including peanut butter, cheese, dyes, flour, inks, milk, and plastics. Carver also developed over a hundred new uses for sweet potatoes, including molasses, postage stamp glue, soap, rubber, and vinegar.

Adhesives	Face ointment	Mock veal cutlet	Rubber
Antiseptic soap	Face powder	Molasses	Rubbing oils
Axle grease	Flavoring paste	Molasses feed	Salad oil
Baby massage cream	Flour	Mucilage	Sandwich vinegar
Bisque powder	Fuel briquettes	Nitroglycerine	Shampoo
Bleach	Glue	Oleomargarine	Shaving cream
Butter from peanut milk	Glycerin	Paints	Shoe polish
Caramel salted peanuts	Goiter treatment	Pancake flour	Sizing for walls
Castoria substitute	Hand lotion	Paper	Soap
Cheese	Ink	Pavement	Soil conditioner
Cheese pimento	Insecticide	Peanut brittle	Stains
Chili sauce	Instant coffee	Peanut butter	Sugar
Chocolate coated peanuts	Insulating boards	Peanut candy bars	Sweeping compound
Chop suey sauce	Iron tonic	Peanut hay meal	Synthetic marble
Cleanser for hands	Laundry soap	Peanut koumiss beverage	Synthetic rubber
Cooking oil	Laxatives	Peanut meat loaf	Talcum powder
Cosmetics	Linoleum	Peanut oil	Tannic acid
Dyes	Mayonnaise	Peanut relish	Tofu sauce
Emulsion for bronchitis	Meal substitutes	Peanut wafers	Tutti frutti
Evaporated peanut beverage	Meat tenderizer	Plastics	Washing powder
Face bleach	Medicine	Pomade for scalp	Wood filler
Face cream	Metal polish	Pomade for skin	Wood stain
Face lotion	Mock chicken	Postage stamp glue	Worcestershire sauce

www.earthlyissues.com/carver.htm   www.black-inventor.com

Environment Friendly Products

Many people have recycled old materials… and created inventions and/or started eco-friendly businesses using very little money.

25 year old invents solar power lamps **for villages in Africa**

Evans Wadongo the winner of 'The Man who changed the world Award'

A Malawian teenager who taught himself how to build a windmill out of junk and bring power to his village. He then went on to build a second, larger windmill to power irrigation pumps. He did this all from books he read in the library.

Remya Jose a 14 year old girl from India invented this pedal operated washing machine. It requires no electricity and using it also gives you exercise. She won a national award for this.

London power station will run on waste fat and produce enough electricity for **40,000 homes.**

Eco-Sikh launches eco-friendly bags

Rahul Tawar

Ludhiana: In a crucial step to spread awareness about the use of eco-friendly plastic bags, members of Eco-Sikh — a US-based environment organization — on Saturday launched compostable bags made out of potato and corn/bio-based starch, to control rising pollution levels aggravated by the use of non-biodeg-

CURB POLLUTION

radable plastic bags across India.

The eco-friendly starch plastic bags were introduced at an event in Gurdwara Sri Dukhniwaran Sahib on Saturday, where heads of all major religions gathered to send out a message of peace and harmony, and create awareness about the use of eco-fri-

CLEAN CITY: Heads of different religious sections along with pollution board members launched compostable bags on Saturday

endly products in day-to-day life. Punjab Pollution Control Board (PPCB) members also shared the stage with Eco-Sikh members and heads of different religious groups.

Eco-Sikh India president Supreet Kaur, while addressing a packed gathering, said:

"Eco-friendly plastic bags are the future, as pollution levels are increasing every day with the use of non-biodegradable plastic bags. These bags play a crucial role in controlling pollution levels across the globe. They have the capability to decompose naturally in 180

days when exposed to water or sunlight, or disposed of in garbage. Even if they are consumed by animals, they are not harmful to them. Moreover, the use of non-biodegradable plastic bags in religious places have increased in the recent past. Because of this, we have started this service from the gurdwara, so that people take this issue seriously, and make an effort to bring these bags into their daily use."

PPCB chief engineer Pradeep Gupta said: "Next month, India is hosting the World Environment Day on 5 June, under the theme 'Beat Plastic Pollution'. PPCB will make efforts to popularize the sale of bio-degradable bags on a large-scale, to overcome rising pollution levels due to the use of plastic bags."

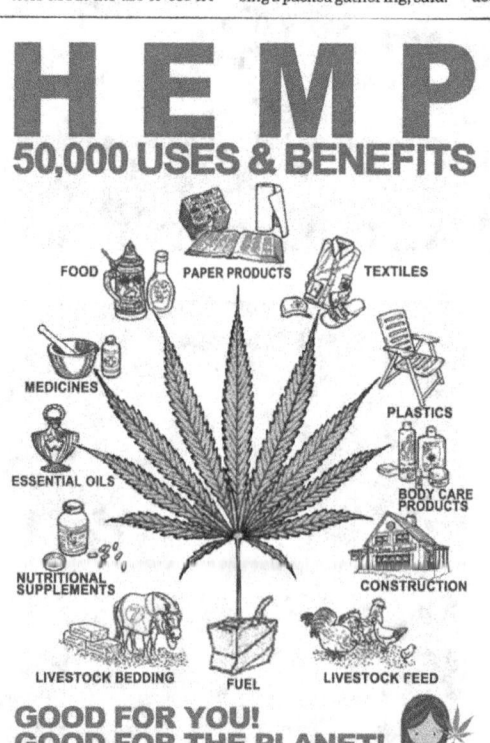

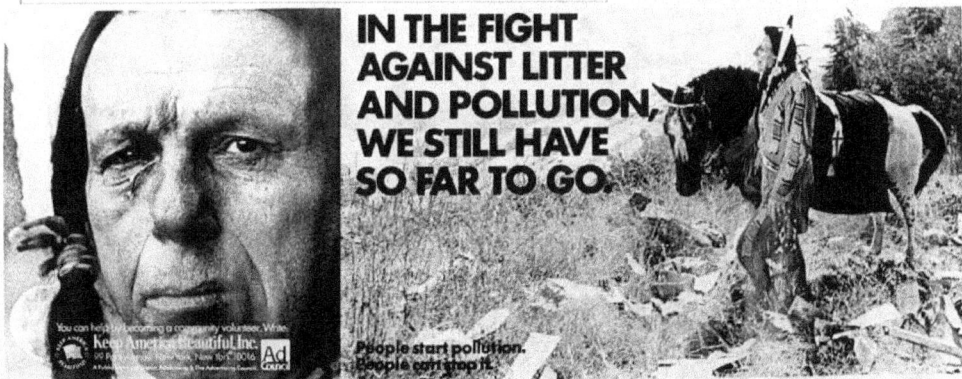

Human activities are the cause of many of our problems...

WE MUST LEARN TO CONTROL WHAT HAPPENS TO WASTE AND
TRASH ...AND TO GET IN TOUCH WITH THAT WHICH BRINGS US
HAPPINESS AND ABUNDANCE.

Change your mind...change your bad habits – and you will be more successful.

Chapter One

*" For the sake of our survival, we must find ways
to transform our skills and occupations into a set
of cleaner, greener, healthier duties — that will help
sustain our health, wealth, and environment."*

IMPROVE YOUR INCOME

CHANGE YOUR MIND... IMPROVE YOUR INCOME...

PLAN YOUR WORK --- THEN WORK YOUR PLAN !

Not long ago our country was run by small businesses---home-based operations that served the needs of their communities. Approximately 60 years ago, more than 75% of the businesses were small—people owned their own enterprises....and the rest were large corporations which hired employees.

Too many people are waiting for that *"big dream job"* to come along. They often ignore the signs of a sluggish economy, avoid any thoughts of starting their own business, and suffer in *"dead-end, low-paying"* jobs. Many of these same people will ignore opportunities to make money from their own business---and turn their noses up at any and all "home-based businesses."

PERHAPS IT IS TIME FOR A CHANGE IN YOUR LIFE !

Even if you are on the right track, you'll get run over if you just sit there.
- Will Rogers

Get Paid
Mo' Money
...

Melvia Miller

WHAT TYPE OF **FUTURE** DO YOU REALLY WANT ????

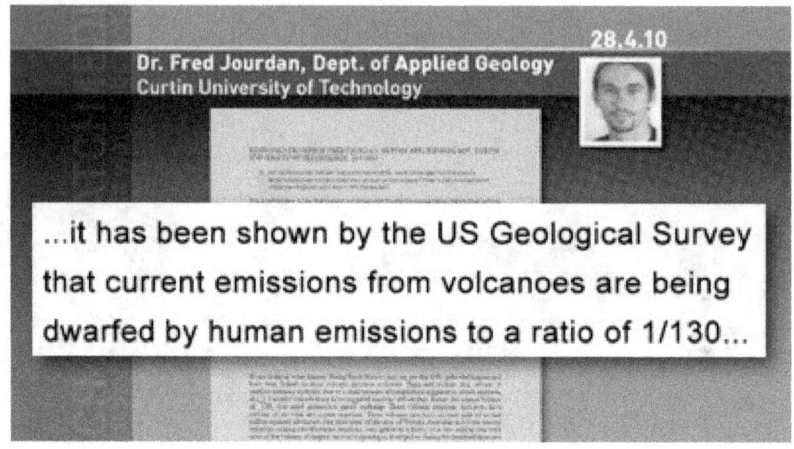

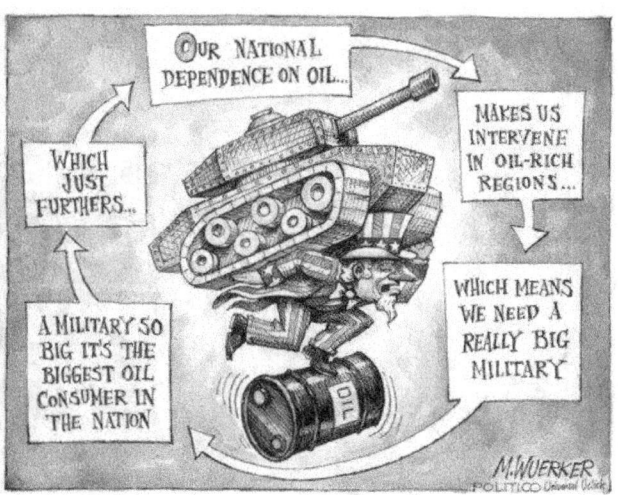

33

Health effects of pollution

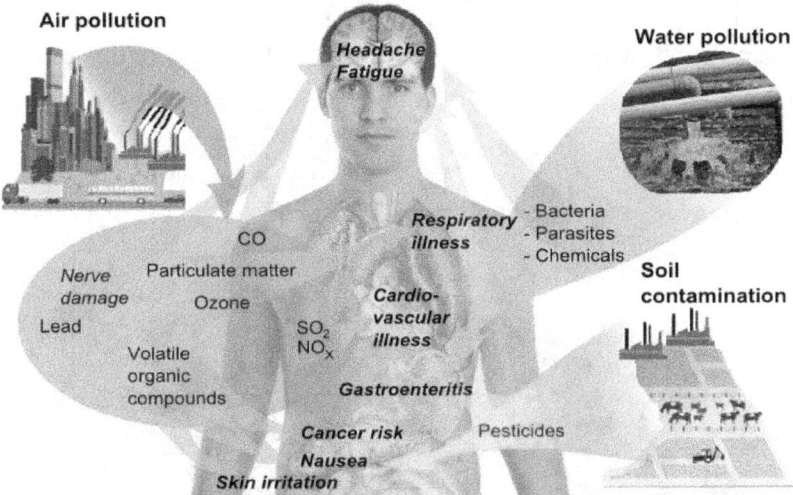

Air pollution

Water pollution

Headache
Fatigue

Respiratory illness
- Bacteria
- Parasites
- Chemicals

CO

Nerve damage

Particulate matter

Ozone

Lead

SO_2
NO_x

Cardio-vascular illness

Soil contamination

Volatile organic compounds

Gastroenteritis

Cancer risk

Pesticides

Nausea

Skin irritation

THE MAIL-STAR Monday, July 22, 1996

Global warming may fuel northward spread of viruses

by MARTY LOGAN
The Canadian Press

Ottawa

The greatest risk of global warming is not flooded coastal cities or dustbowl prairies but the growth and spread of killer diseases such as malaria, says an Ottawa scientist.

A temperature increase of just one-half degree Celsius could cause a staggering 80-120 million more cases of malaria as mosquitoes carrying the disease spread throughout Africa and Central and South America, says John Last, professor emeritus in the department of epidemiology at the University of Ottawa. "That's a hell of a lot more than are going to die of heat stroke in cities like Shanghai and Beijing and various other places," Last said recently.

In 1993 about two million people died of malaria. There were 300-500 million cases reported worldwide.

Infectious diseases kill 17 million people every year and are the world's leading cause of death, says a 1996 report by the World Health Organization.

So-called greenhouse gases such as carbon dioxide are believed responsible for global warming: trapping heat and raising temperatures within the earth's atmosphere.

Although North America wouldn't be hit as hard as warmer climates, Canadians could expect more cases of equine encephalitis, also known as sleeping sickness, said Last, who recently worked as a consultant for the WHO.

The mosquito-borne virus frequently attacks the brain and central nervous system of farm animals. During a 1963 outbreak in Manitoba it killed two people. Sixteen others were diagnosed with the disease.

Sleeping sickness wouldn't be a huge threat to people but "could have a pretty devastating economic impact," Last said.

Another danger is dengue, one of two sicknesses that have reached epidemic proportions in South America and could threaten North America, an infectious disease specialist told the Krever inquiry into tainted blood last year.

The other notable disease is cholera, the specialist said.

Assessing the possible danger of infectious disease to Canadians requires greater co-operation between health and climate researchers, says Environment Canada climatologist Abdel Maarouf.

In the meantime, people everywhere can take appropriate measures to reduce the risk. In the developing world those include vaccination and water purification, said Maarouf.

Like many of us, viruses and their hosts have become international travellers. The aggressive Asian tiger mosquito — carrier of 15 diseases — stowed away on a load of old tires in Japan for its trip to North America a few years ago.

It's now in some northern states and there are fears the insect could soon arrive in Canada.

"People when they are travelling in infected areas have to take extra care about where they are going and where they are coming from," Maarouf said.

According to Last, during the 1993 Ebola outbreak in Zaire a French reporter entered the contaminated area then left the country without a check-up. When she arrived in Switzerland the woman was sick.

Authorities feared an Ebola outbreak in Europe, but the reporter was diagnosed with malaria.

Last is optimistic about the future of human beings.

"We're a resilient species, a resourceful species, an intelligent species. We're very adaptable and we have demonstrated pretty convincingly that we can live in all kinds of harsh environmental circumstances."

Habitats are destroyed by . . .

- **Air pollution** effects the air we breathe.
- Plants and animals need clean air.
- Factories and cars put harmful smoke and fumes in our air.
- Air pollution causes major damage to our health and the environment.

Forests are nature's air cleaner. We need forest to help keep the air clean.

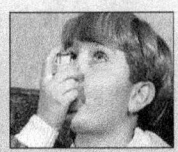

NOTE: If you do your *due diligence*…research it… you will find that most of the environmental problems (air and water pollution) are caused by greedy, callous, neglectful human activities**.**

The early 1900's Lohner-Porsche, originally electric-powered, then with an internal combustion engine powering hub-mounted electric motors.

A BETTER FUTURE REQUIRES THAT WE CHANGE OUR BAD HABITS.

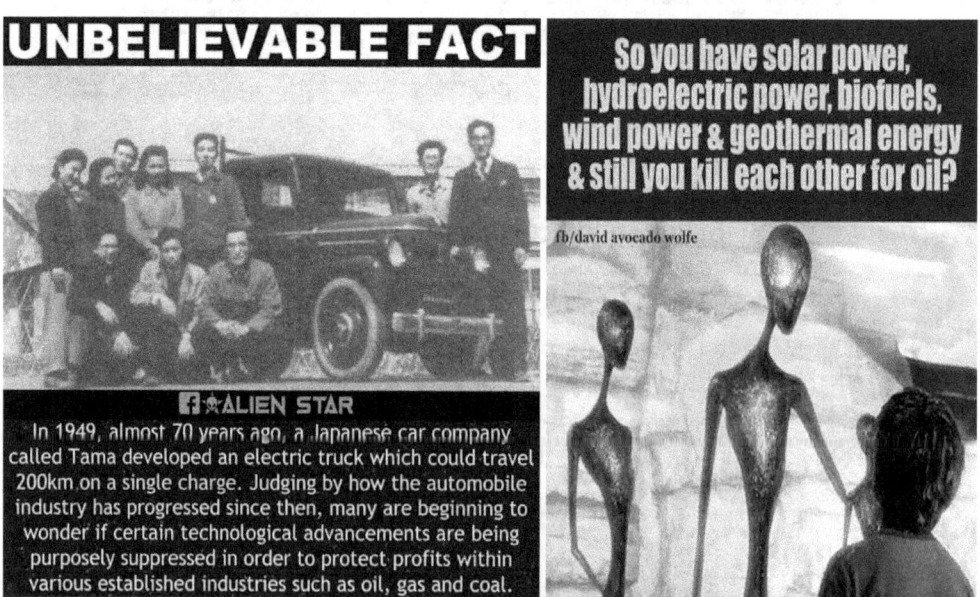

UNBELIEVABLE FACT

f ✭ALIEN STAR

In 1949, almost 70 years ago, a Japanese car company called Tama developed an electric truck which could travel 200km on a single charge. Judging by how the automobile industry has progressed since then, many are beginning to wonder if certain technological advancements are being purposely suppressed in order to protect profits within various established industries such as oil, gas and coal.

So you have solar power, hydroelectric power, biofuels, wind power & geothermal energy & still you kill each other for oil?

fb/david avocado wolfe

Who would act to increase **pollution** for profit$ …???

Water Succeeds Gasoline As New Invention Is Perfected

WATER powered automobiles are predicted for the not too distant future as the result of an invention of G. H. Garrett of Dallas, Texas, which substitutes water for gasoline.

Garrett uses an electrolytic carburetor which breaks up water by electrolysis into its component gases, hydrogen and oxygen, and then forces the explosive hydrogen into the combustion chambers for fuel.

For operating the automobile motor on which the tests have been conducted, Garrett has added an over-size generator to supply the extra electricity needed by the carburetor. Beyond that, the motor has needed no changes, though it has been in operation continuously for several days.

Garrett has protected his device with patents.

This water powered motor is the invention of G. H. Garrett, who is shown here with his right hand upon the electrolytic carburetor which obtains explosive hydrogen from water.

STANLEY MEYER

THE MOST FAMOUS WATER CAR INVENTOR.

Something has gone terribly wrong with our present economic and political system. Millions of jobs have been lost – while WALL STREET gets richer and richer. And some politicians continue to set up a tax code and other regulations that benefit the rich.... and those agencies that are drugging and polluting the environment.

CURRENT FORM OF CAPITALISM = * (Crap-italism)

This whale washed up dead on a British beach. In its stomach … the remains of 23 plastic bags

www.wilderness.org   www.350.org   www.coolearth.org

www.greenpeace.org/usa   www.plasticoceans.org

"If the bee disappears from the surface of the earth, man would have no more than four years to live."

- Albert Einstein

THE SCIENTIFIC DEBATE ON GLOBAL WARMING IS OVER.

The most comprehensive study to date has found

97%

of published climate papers with a position on human-caused global warming AGREE

GLOBAL WARMING IS REAL, AND WE ARE THE CAUSE.

TheConsensusProject.com

Chapter Two

Solve your own problems via *Going Green*

ECO-FRIENDLY PRODUCTS AND SERVICES

GO GREEN... to earn & save more $$$

SAVE MONEY BY GREENING YOUR HOME:

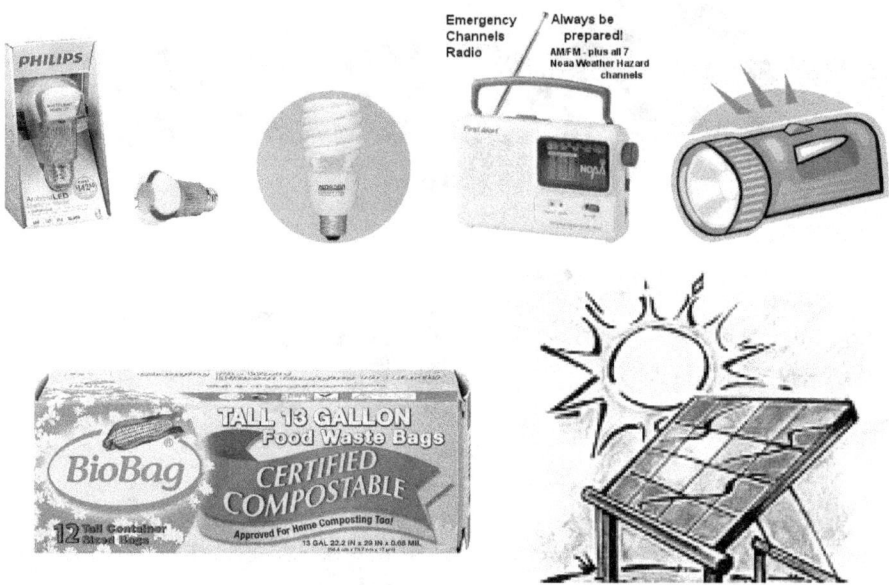

You no longer have to pay huge fees to get SOLAR PANELS. Some companies will lease them to you at reasonable fees.... such as: www.sungevity.com

BEGIN AT HOME

STAY AWAY FROM USING CHEMICALS, TOXIC SUBSTANCES, AND GM FOODS ... AS MUCH AS POSSIBLE...

- Chemical pesticides & fertilizers can be very harmful to humans, pets, and plants....causing sicknesses – or poisoning.
- Chemical pesticides are killing off the bees, which pollinate plants so that we can have food, flowers, and reproduction of plants.
- Some pesticides & fertilizers are made from fossil fuels...and tend to embed into the soil and our food... and are extremely harmful.

YOU CAN BEGIN A HEALTHIER, CLEANER LIFESTYLE – *naturally* !

SOAPS and more for PERSONAL CARE...

NATURAL HOUSEHOLD CLEANERS

Natural, homemade cleaning products offer a non-toxic and earth-friendly solution to your cleaning dilemmas. One of the best things to have in your green cleaning tote comes from an easily available citrus fruit. Lemons and lemon juice have a number of natural and effective cleaning applications and will leave your home clean and fresh. Dis-infect, deodorize, whiten or cut through grease and grime with the power of natural citrus fruit. You may wish to wear gloves when handling pure citrus solvents to avoid skin irritation.

Citrus formulas are excellent also for getting rid of grease, grime, and old scum. Every place you use these cleaners will smell much better... and will be healthier and cleaner. Lemons are acidic and can provide some antibacterial and antiseptic properties. The more **orange** and/or **lemon**....the better it will clean.

Use to clean dirty carpets & showers.... greasy ovens and stoves.... add to laundry detergent.... Wash walls, floors, and doors.... get rid of oil in driveways....and detail automobiles....

MAKE YOUR OWN CITRIS CLEANERS & DETERGENTS ....

HOW TO CLEAN DIRTY STOVES

This tip takes a bit long time but once you make this solution, cleaning will be very easy. All you have to do is fill a jar with lemon peels, add vinegar to cover the peels. Seal with tight-fitting lid. Put it away and forget about it for two weeks.After two weeks, drain half of the vingar and fill the rest with water. Use this solution to get rid of greasiest stoves

info@saleeqa.com

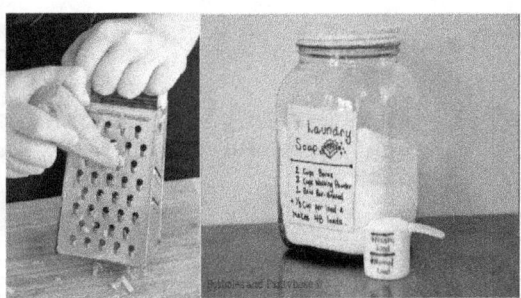

Make your own natural laundry detergent too !

What you'll need to make your very own **Laundry DETERGENT....**

    1 Bar (5.5 oz approx.) **Fels-Naptha**, **Zote** Soap or **Ivory** Soap
    2 Cups Arm & Hammer *"Super Washing Soda*
    2 Cups **Borax**

Instructions: CUT THE BAR SOAP into small pieces and then use a food **grater/chopper** ...or **Blender/Food Processor....** adding all ingredients to prepare the detergent.

EASY TO MAKE NON-TOXIC INSECTICIDES:

1) Use 2 tsp. of liquid dishwashing soap in a quart of water.

   (a) Put in a spray bottle and use on indoor plants.
   (b) Add a chopped garlic, onion and baking soda for a stronger spray.

2) For outdoor plants in a garden…to get rid of spider mites, cabbage worms, and similar pests –

   (a) Put 2 tbsp. of SEA SALT in a gallon of water
   (b) Use spray bottle to put this mixture on garden plants.
   (c) Add a 2 tsps. of cornstarch with Neem Oil.

3) To kill BED BUGS….

   (a)   Spray bed bugs with rubbing alcohol. This kills them on
   the spot. Use a dish brush to kill the visible eggs.

DIY Bed Bug Spray

Mattresses & Pillows are often ignored. Here
is an easy & effective way to keep your space
critter free! Don't forget to take it with you
whenever you travel.

- 25 drops Eucalyptus
- 10 drops Purification
- 10 drops Thieves

Place oil drops in a 2 oz amber glass spray
bottle, fill remaining bottle with distilled water.
Shake before use. Spray mattress & pillows
every time you change the sheets.

Compiled by PESTKILL.ORG

(b)   **Steam**
also kills all bedbugs and the eggs.   Set up a way to create steam in
your home. Use a small handhold steam cleaner to steam your bed
including frame, bed boards, mattress and let it dry. Grind up some
crystal silica gel and apply it all over in your bed room. Put some on
your mattress, around the bed and along the wall. The fine silica gel
stuck to the bug cannot be shaken off, causing it to dehydrate and die.

www.bed-bugs.net   www.livingwithbugs.com/natural_pesticides.html

LEMON EUCALYPTUS OIL

LAVENDER OIL

CITRONELLA OIL

CATNIP

CINNAMON OIL

PEPPERMINT

NEEM

THYME

TEA TREE OIL

NATURAL **MOSQUITO REPELLENTS** THAT REALLY WORK

Top10 Home Remedies
To explore more, visit
www.Top10HomeRemedies.com

For ORGANIC Gardening

Garden Safe

Bt Worm & Caterpillar KILLER

Use on Edible Plants up to Day of Harvest

MICE HATE PEPPERMINT:

Irritates their nose

Hides Pheromone Trails

5 ways to use it:

1. drops of oil on cotton balls
2. mix oil with cleaner
3. mix oil with water in a spray bottle
4. plant mint around your house
5. buy a mint-based mouse repellent

When and where possible buy non-chemically based insecticides ….and/ or mix your own via using herbs, fruits, essential oils, and other natural ingredients.

…Repel Spiders Naturally

Do you want to know how to get rid of spiders? Do you want to repel spiders or to kill spiders? If you want a spider repellent, here is a

natural spider repellent recipe for you! You can repel spiders so they don't return.

Keep Spiders OUT of your house! Make a mixture using either lemon or orange *Essential Oil* and spray it across all your doorsteps and window sills. Re-apply once a week or so just to keep spiders out of your house. They won't cross this barrier because as soon as they taste the orange or lemon essential oil, it will repel spiders naturally!

Add lemons and **BAKING SODA** & **BORAX...** and you also have an excellent cleaning agent.

GET RID OF ROACHES

Take an old CLEAN plastic margarine container or *'Cool Whip'* container cut a quarter size hole in the bowl right at the rim. Do not cut the lid but retain the lid for later use. IF the container is going to be inside you can cut up to four holes. IF the container is going to be placed outside your home only cut one hole to protect the bait from the elements.

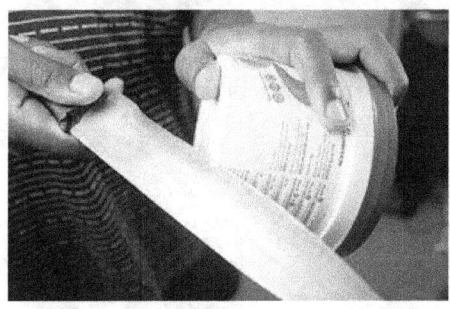  

Using a bucket or washable glass bowl, mix one cup common household BORAX, 1/2 cup bacon grease, and 1/2 cup sugar. Add honey or more bacon grease to make the mixture moist enough to form into balls.

Using plastic gloves....Form the mixture into large balls.

Snap the top into place.(the TOP- which was originally the bottom)

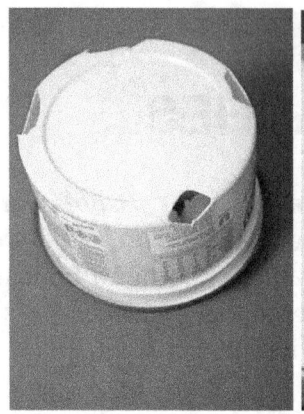 

Set into place inside cupboards -- behind appliances and even outside in the garden to safely rid the area of ants and cockroaches before they enter your home without harming the environment or spraying harmful chemical pesticides.

****

Dissolve Dog Poop !

One way to do it is to scoop... but there are also ways to dissolve poop. Several products which can be applied to the poop ... causing it to dissolve... are available at PET STORES and other major stores.

Sanitation is important for everyone's health.... so we must get rid of critter poop that gets deposited in your yard. You can **mix up** your own formulas – using non-chemical cleaning products (safe for pets and children) that contain at least a few of these ingredients: *enzymes, oxygen, citrus (lemon and lime), vinegar, and baking soda.

Donate to Goodwill. Reduce. Reuse. Recycle.

We are like tenant farmers
chopping down the fence
around our house for fuel
when we should be using
Nature's inexhaustible sources
of energy — sun, wind and tide.
I'd put my money on the sun
and solar energy. What a source
of power! I hope we don't have
to wait until oil and coal run out
before we tackle that.

• Thomas Alva Edison, 1931

Words of Wisdom

In less than 15 seconds -- the sun
emits enough energy to power the
whole world for a full day.

~ Scientific Fact

LIVE SIMPLY SO THAT
OTHERS MAY SIMPLY LIVE

quotesarcade.com

Unfortunately, the old form of "capitalism" has become more like a Ponzi *(pyramid)* scheme (scam) – where only the top 2% earn 95% of the money and the rest of the people are left to struggle for left-overs... and suffer from the bad policies that are destroying the environment – for profits.

Main Street burns up while Wall Street gets bailed out.

*WE NEED TO CREATE A **NEW** TYPE OF ECONOMY...*

ACTION IS NEEDED TO HELP IMPROVE OUR WORLD...

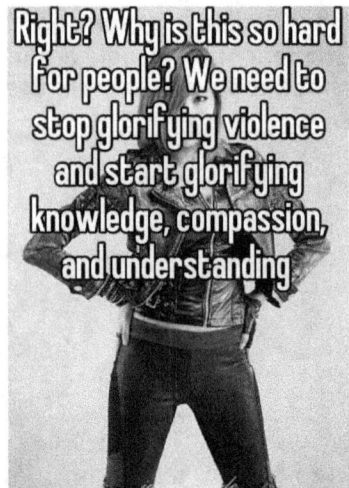

Right? Why is this so hard for people? We need to stop glorifying violence and start glorifying knowledge, compassion, and understanding

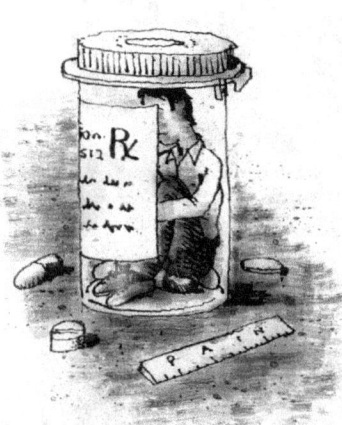

HELP OTHERS AND YOU WILL BE HELPED

Money can't buy you happiness...

Lifeisajoke.com

...but it does bring you a more pleasant form of misery -Spike Milligan

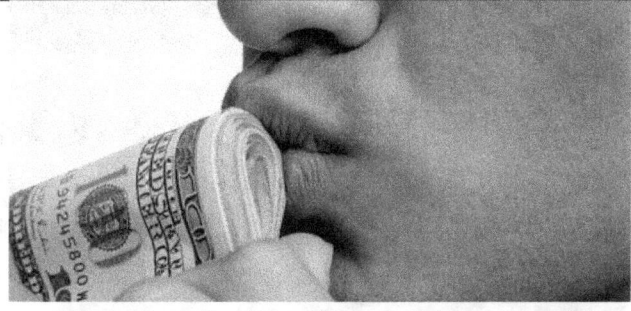

Use funds for the public good !

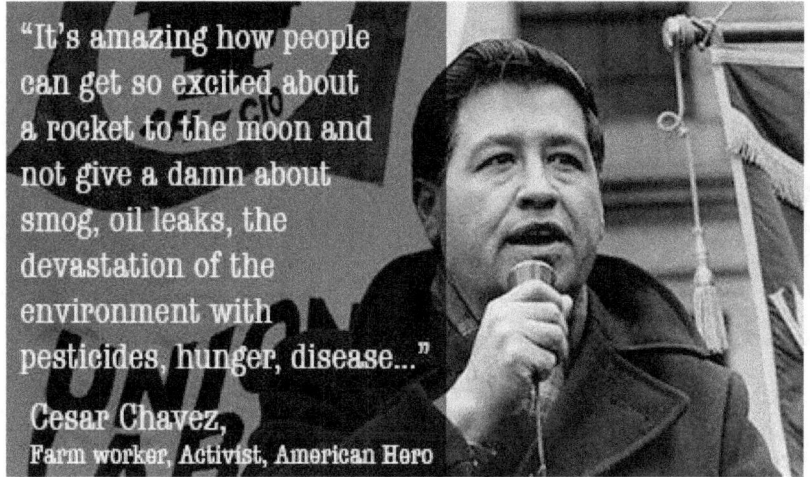

"It's amazing how people can get so excited about a rocket to the moon and not give a damn about smog, oil leaks, the devastation of the environment with pesticides, hunger, disease..."

Cesar Chavez,
Farm worker, Activist, American Hero

35 MILLION PEOPLE IN AMERICA FACE HUNGER EACH YEAR

96 BILLION POUNDS OF FOOD GOES TO WASTE

pov·er·ty is deprivation of common necessities that determine the quality of life, including food, clothing, shelter and safe drinking water, and may also include the deprivation of opportunities to learn, and/or to obtain better employment to escape poverty.

Could you live like that?

Solving Pov·er·ty

· Are you helping? ·

WANT TO SEE A BETTER WORLD ?

START WITH THE PERSON IN THE MIRROR!

ENJOY *Capitalism*

SUNFLOWER FARMERS MARKET

KICK CHILDHOOD OBESITY

"Cease to be a drudge, seek to be an artist."
~ Mary McLeod Bethune

Start a Business

Together We Can Save Our **Only Home**

Intervention For Existence (Heal earth Team)

If you are feeling angry, disappointed, frustrated or powerless – you can change that. The power to alter your life lies mostly in your own hands. Start taking action to find ways to change whatever is impeding your progress. We are all in need of "new leases on life."

One great thing about the United States is that virtually anybody can go out and start a small business. All it takes is some "know how" and some hard work. While having a lot of money helps, you can start a business with little or no <u>capital</u>.

<u>KEYS TO MAKING MONEY:</u>

One main key to making these types of business work is to find a system that creates a "win-win" situation for both the client and the business owners. Wealth is created by marketing a valuable product or service that fulfills a need or desire to mass numbers of people. Invest in the future of a clean, healthy **GREEN** PLANET—renewable energy, new eco-products, recycling services, and/or holistic health products, etc. The "green businesses," and the people they employ, will be doing important work that will point the way to a clean, healthier, green sustainable **ECO-FRIENDLY** future.

CREATE NEW WAYS TO USE YOUR SKILLS --

Do you have a skill or talent that you can use to create products or services? Can you type well? Are you a good baker? …musician?....mechanic?

Find sources to purchase low cost (wholesale) products, which you can sell. Try: GARAGE and RUMMAGE SALES—or perhaps booth-sales at school events…. OR -- Set up a website or an **EBAY** account to offer what you have.

Also, check with your local churches, Chamber of Commerce, and other business services. They often offer FLEA MARKETS, networking events, and other fairs where you can rent a booth to sell your wares. Offer coupons, free gifts… or hold raffles or give out door prizes to attract more interest and also promote your wares.

WOULD YOU LIKE TO KNOW WHERE TO SELL YOUR PRODUCTS & SERVICES ?

Just look around any place that you go--- schools, clinics, hospitals, office buildings,hotels, etc.----and guess where they get the various plaques, bags, health products, clothing, uniforms, ashtrays, dishes, light bulbs, cleaning products, decorations, furniture, supplies, machinery, (and so on)…

Where do you think city hall or the schools purchase some of their office supplies, books, decorations, art, and other products?

…… *ANSWER = …they buy from small businesses.

WHY GO GREEN ?

"*Going GREEN*" has many connotations, such as -- living frugally out in the woods without modern luxury. Or some have defined it as *"becoming a nature fanatic"* and thus, not using any types of technology. And there are others who believe that our climate will collapse if nations fail to clean up our toxic pollution.

There are many skeptics when global warming is mentioned, or on the other hand, people are just lazy and think that it will all be OK, or they can just leave the problem up to others or the government to fix.

No matter who you are, or on what side of life's fence, here is a challenge for you:

Whatever your political or religious persuasion--it does not matter if you are an environmentalist, a housewife, student, mechanic, teacher, a successful capitalist, a national park association or a corporation – there are legitimate, solid reasons to start living sustainably --- within the world's limits.

REASONS TO GO GREEN:

- It will help cut your energy costs.
(using solar power or bio-fuels is economical)
- Gain a competitive edge via higher quality, healthier products.
- Increase health by using non-toxic, polluting products.
- Produce less trash and waste – recycle.
- Decrease amount of poison chemicals in the water.
- Help decrease dependency on foreign oil.
- Eco-friendly homes and products have more value.
- Support groups that help protect our environment.
- Stop dumping harmful chemicals in the air & water.
- Share the income with others in a "co-op" manner.

- *HELP TO* -- **Create a new cleaner, sustainable economy.**

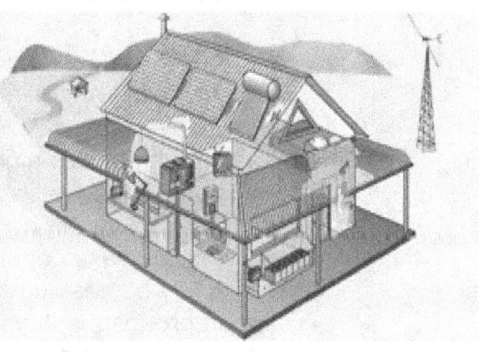

MAIL ORDER MARKETING 101

Not long ago, our country was filled with primarily small businesses that served the needs of their communities. Approximately 60 years ago, huge corporate entities did not run the nation or exert heavy (biased) influence upon the U.S. Congress. Back then, companies were growing and there was **not** a lot of fear of "lay-offs" because most people worked for themselves or within a growing medium-size company.

After a while, as companies grew, people began to move to the big cities – and more and more -- they worked for the big corporations. The U.S. went through more than 40 years of growth in technology. The size of companies continued to grow – and for the most part, the smaller businesses slowly disappeared. Technology, computers and micro-chips changed the way we all live and do business. And now in the 21st century – we are experiencing one of the worst economic recessions in history. Ironically, those at the top continue to get richer....as 75% of the people struggle to pay bills.

Unfortunately, the major corporations have become more and more inclined to mechanize and seek cheap-labor. Many people with college degrees and high-level training are finding themselves under-paid and over-worked. As people struggle to find new ways of earning income – small and home-based businesses are making a come-back. Get involved with services or activities that you enjoy. **Be creative !**

101 Fantastic Gift Basket Ideas

Holiday Fun

www.globalgoodspartners.org   www.worldofgood.com

www.humanitystore.org   www.WOCF.ws   www.greenandmore.com

SUCCESS HAPPENS WHEN PREPARATION MEETS OPPORTUNITY.
WE CAN SOLVE THE MOST DANGEROUS PROBLEMS THAT
THREATEN OUR WORLD – (UNEMPLOYMENT AND CLIMATE
CHANGE DISASTERS) BY USING CLEANER, GREENER,
NATURAL, **ECO-FRIENDLY** PRODUCTS.

STARTING YOUR OWN MAIL ORDER BUSINESS MAY BE A SOLUTION TO SOME OF YOUR PROBLEMS TOO !

It is easy to start such a business... all you need is:

- A place to work – kitchen, den, garage, basement.
- A phone and answering machine.
- File cabinet, folders, envelopes & other office supplies.
- Access to a photocopy machine, computer, word processor, typewriter, etc.
- A **P.O. Box** or other **business address** to receive mail.
- A small budget for stamps, printing, ink, paper, and other necessities.

Most of us have received a brochure, newsletter, flyer, post-card, or catalog in the mail which invites us to buy something. The people who are sending out these materials have discovered ways to earn money via the mail. MAIL ORDER sales can be very profitable.

BASIC STEPS FOR GETTING STARTED:

A) Choose a catchy business name.

B) Organize your work-area so that you can file your records, use the computer, and keep track of incoming mail, etc.

C) Make a **PLAN** – outlining what you will offer – type of products & services.

D) Select products that you want to offer.

E) Find low cost newspapers, magazines, etc.—where you can place inexpensive ads.

F) Set up a system for filling orders received.

G) Keep good records of sales and expenses.

If you want to work from home, running a lucrative business that costs little to start and requires no specialized skills – **MAIL ORDER** may be for you. Working from a kitchen table, you can take orders, process payments, and dispatch shipments picked up by a parcel service from a remote warehouse run by yet another vendor.

PRODUCTS ARE AVAILABLE THRU COMPANIES THAT OFFER DROP-SHIPPING SERVICES. ALL YOU DO IS GET THE ORDERS.

www.ecomall.com/biz/wholes.htm   www.dropshippingcentral.com

FLYERS, BROCHURES & ORDER FORMS

If you are able to type and write well, and have access to a computer with a word-processor, you can easily make your own flyers, order forms, or a NEWSLETTER.

IT IS IMPORTANT that your flyers, letters, post-cards, or any printed materials that you mail out give a good impression. If they look like cheap junk, most people will treat them like that and throw the information away.

If you are not able to make your own, find inexpensive ways to have them made. You can also order return-address labels and other office supplies – so that they look decent. If you have a website, include that on your printed materials also.

Make it simple and easy for customers to order. Include an **ORDER FORM**…or instructions on how to place orders.

Order form	print, fill out, mail with check.		
Item	Each	Quantity	Amount
Missouri (only) sales tax 6.075%			
Postage $ 5 US, $12 outside US			
		Total	
Ship to Name:			
Address:			
City State Zip:			

make checks payable to Science & Humanities Press
P.O. Box 7151, Chesterfield, MO 63006-7151
(636) 394-4950
www.banis-associates.com
E-mail: banis@banis-associates.com

Sources for IMPRINTED, PERSONALIZED… free and low cost business cards, post cards, calendars & stationery --

www.wdrake.com   www.vistaprint.com

WRITE & PUBLISH ... ads, newsletters and/or **books --**

BRIEF LIST OF SUCCESS TIPS FOR WRITERS:

* Study and examine the successful publications created by other writers...such as: *"HARRY POTTER"* books ... writers like Stephen King, Alex Haley, Robert Kyosaki, and Maya Angelou....and other "best sellers." Seek to find out -- What are these writers doing that leads to success? What is their writing style that is so appealing? How are they advertising their books that helps create sales ?

* Read magazines and other publications designed to help writers--- such as: WRITERS DIGEST and POETS & WRITERS MAGAZINE. These types of publications are filled with valuable tips and resources for writers.

* **Write about subjects in a new and refreshing way**-- from a different angle or viewpoint. Create a new "angle" --- amazing real-life stories, odd characters, action or other unique ways... for presenting topics. **The same techniques** are necessary for writing any type of ads or promotional materials for a business. * Create a way to **STAND OUT !**

BUY & PROMOTE BOOKS or ... MARKET YOUR OWN PRODUCTS & SERVICES

You can promote your newsletter or any other products that you may want to sell online....at low cost or free.

ONLINE SITES WHERE YOU CAN PLACE **FREE** ADS:

www.tradekey.com   www.usfreeads.com

www.PRWeb.com   www.bestwayclassifieds.com

www.listings.yellowpages.com   www.add-your-biz.com

www.greenapplicator.com   www.freeadsplanet.com

www.freeclassifiedadsonline.com   www.global-free-classified-ads.com

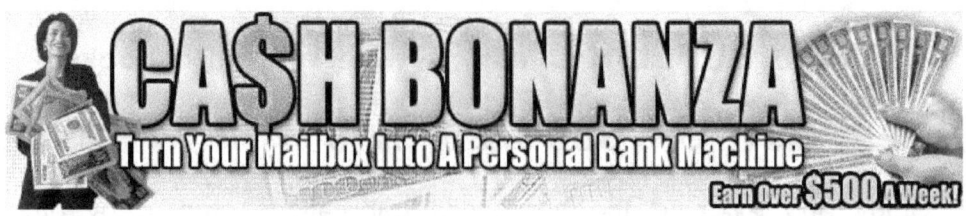

IMPORTANCE OF MARKETING ...

Networking is a concept that involves meeting other people, exchanging business info, helping each other, and getting the word out about whatever services or products you offer---and meeting people who may be of assistance or who may become customers. When you attend conferences, meetings, or join clubs---get out and talk to people, give them your business cards, flyers and e-mail address – contact information.

OFFER SOMETHING THAT PEOPLE WANT ENJOY, AND DESIRE --- take action to do something that is a good service to others -- and help other people, help solve problems, help our planet .... and you will meet with success.

Keys to Success:

REMEMBER: *"A fool and money are soon parted."*
Good money management is essential to achieving &
maintaining success.

* **Waste not--- want not**. SAVE & INVEST the money that
you do have...

OFFER SOMETHING valuable, unique, and beneficial to others.

* Invest in real estate, stocks, bonds, retirement funds, and
other financial vehicles that help you build equity and value.

* **Seek resources** *(companies, suppliers, merchandisers, catalogs,
distributors, etc.)* which permit you to buy products & services at
discount, wholesale and low prices...and those the create ***"residual
income."*** *(i.e. -- long term commissions or royalties)*

* Rewards are determined by the problems you help others solve.
Businesses or services that help solve problems are in demand.

* The quality of your preparation determines the quality of your
performance.

* *Plan your work---then work your plan.*

* **SUCCESS** occurs when proper training & preparation meet
with opportunity.

* Your daily habits help build -(or destroy) your future.

* *Practice makes perfect.*

Dr. Richard Ryan of The <u>University of Rochester</u> reports what we all have been savvy to for awhile now -- that seeing naturescapes helps reduces stress, and even having a <u>window</u> in a hospital room helps people recover more quickly. *"While the salubrious effects of nature are well documented... this study shows that the benefits include reducing antagonistic attitudes and relieving stress. Exposure to natural as opposed to man-made environments leads people to value community and close relationships and to be more generous with money,"* stated Dr. Richard Ryan and his team of researchers at the University of Rochester.   **www.ways2achieve.com**

Chapter Three

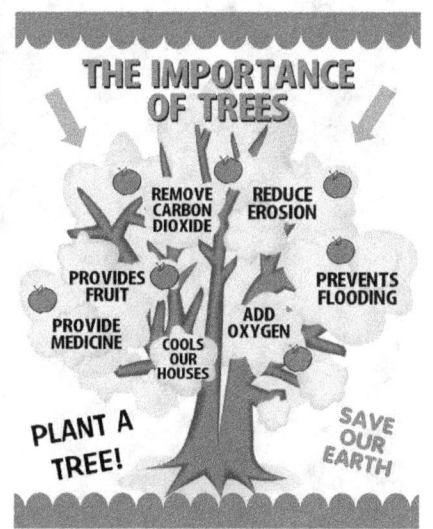

GO BIG in a **Green** Business

"Get in tune with Nature's senses. The more we can open up and connect with these senses, the more we heal, rejuvenate and are inspired."

~ **Dr. Mike Cohen** *(Eco-pyschologist)*, author of
<u>*"Reconnecting with Nature"*</u>

FOUNTAINS OF YOUTH

Thousands of years ago, African ancestors believed that NATURE offered what was needed to keep us well physically, mentally emotionally, and spiritually. Honoring **Earth's laws** and using what Nature offers ... are some of the oldest techniques used for health care and they are claimed to predate all organized religions. The ancient *'medicine men'* of **the oldest societies** used many forms of medicines, treatments, therapies, and even surgery long ago.

WATER still holds a special place in most religions and cultures today. It has been used as in ceremonies, for ablution, for baptisms, and for many other rituals...because without water – there can be no life as we know it.

Words of Wisdom

"When a man moves away from Nature his heart becomes hard."

~ Ancient African Proverb

Words of Wisdom

"We learned to be patient observers like the owl. We learned cleverness from the crow, and courage from the eagle. We must protect the forests for those who can't speak for themselves such as the birds, animals, fish and trees."

~ Native American Philosophy

learn earth science

SCIENCE

GO BIG in a **Green** *Enterprise*

Successful green businesses not only benefit the environment, but also use green business practices as means to market their products. Economic experts predict that the "green economy" will offer several ways to boost job creation, and help reduce pollution and impede eco-destruction.

According to the *The Organic Trade Association's* Manufacturer Survey, the organic industry grew by 21% to reach $17.7 billion in consumer sales in 2006. Over the last decade organic sales have increase by an average of 20%, and this rate is expected to remain steady over the next 20 years. The explosion of organic and eco-friendly products on retail store shelves is more than just a passing fad. It's big business. This means big opportunities for environmentally minded entrepreneurs. If you are thinking of starting a green business, consider the following **tips:**

Find Your Niche. As the natural, organic lifestyle continues to catch on with consumers, there are many growth possibilities. Products such as food, cosmetics and cleaning supplies are growing areas within the organic trade. Or you may want to learn to build SOLAR PANELS, or to invest in new "energy-saving" light bulbs, bio-fuels — or clothing made from recycled items….or any of the new products that are on the market.

RESEARCH…and find high quality – desirable products.

www.greenpeople.org   www.cleangreenbiz.com   www.realgoods.com

CLEAN ENERGY FOR AMERICA

POWER UP AMERICA

** ECO -- is a very meaningful "prefix" to words ---

WELL MIND = GOOD ECO-PSYCHE

-- which leads to HEALTHY ECO-LOGY...

and will help us all ECO-NOMICALLY !

SOURCES FOR GREEN JOBS = www.greenjobsfree.com   **www.greenforall.org**

www.beagreenirene.com   www.ecotraining.com

www.veteransgreenjobs.org   www.environmentalcareer.com

www.4edutainment.webs.com   www.WOCF.ws/Ecology

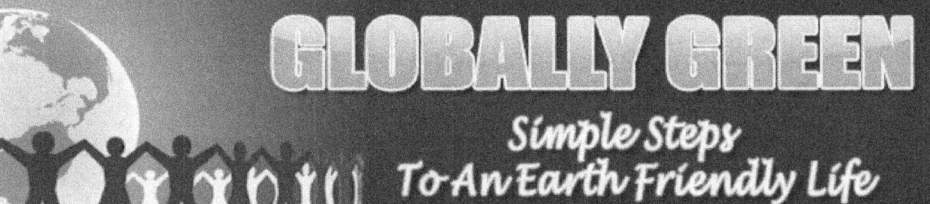

EARN MONEY RECYCLING --

SELL YOUR OLD CELL PHONE, IPAD, and other used devices & jewelry !

www.getgreentogetgreen.com   www.SellCell.com   www.hellototem.com

www.recyclebank.com   www.grc**recycling**.com

www.earth911.com/news/2010/04/05/**get**-**money**-for-**recycling**

www.greenamerica.org/**get**paid4**recycling**

www.thepennyhoarder.com/2011/09/5-weird-ways-to-make-money-recycling

----

POLLUTION AND CLIMATE CHANGE HAVE CAUSED MANY FOOD PROBLEMS.

It means a big mountain of rotting trash.

Food waste accounts for nearly 15% of American landfills, according to the EPA.

All that food is rotting, and rotting food produces methane, a powerful greenhouse gas.

Food Recovery groups work to unite volunteers, college students (etc.) to fight **food** waste and hunger by recovering surplus perishable **food** from their campuses, cafes, and businesses to distribute to people who need food.

The Food Recovery Network is a network of student groups at four different colleges in America. We recover surplus food from campus dining halls and sporting events that would otherwise be thrown away and instead, take the food to local homeless shelters. We hope to ignite a food recovery movement, expand the Food Recovery Network .... www.foodrecoverynetwork.org

BUSINESS PLANS & PROPOSALS

Paths to the big buck$

Business Start-Up Checklist

Below is a listing of the steps neccesary to create a business ---

Determine the Business Type

Now that you've decided to start a business, you need to decide what type of business. Businesses generally fall into three categories:

1. **Service:** Will the company provide a service? Examples include lawn care companies, law and accounting firms, and hair salons.
2. **Retail** (Merchandising): Will the company sell products in small quantities directly to the consumer? Examples include grocery, hardware, and stationery stores.
3. **Manufacturing:** Will the company create a product from raw materials or pre-fabricated components? Examples include car and computer manufacturers, and construction firms.

Determine the Ownership Structure --

Careful consideration should be given to a company's legal structure.

Some questions to ask:

- Who and How many owners will there be?
- How important is it to limit personal liability for debts or claims against the business? In general, incorporating is the best means of limiting liability.
- Which business structure will result in the lowest taxes? There is no universal answer to this question. Tax-wise, however, some structures are better than others.

CONTENTS OF A GOOD BUSINESS PLAN ---

The content is more important than the length. Your **Business Plan** can be as short as 10 pages or as long as 300 pages, but the essential aspect of a GOOD PLAN is that it clearly explains, outlines, and analyzes how the corporation will operate.

At the very least, a BUSINESS PLAN should explain the following:

* GOALS & PURPOSES OF THE BUSINESS

* MISSION STATEMENT

* GENERAL DESCRIPTION OF THE OPERATIONS

* LOCATION OF THE BUSINESS...SATELLITE OFFICES, etc.

* STRUCTURE OF THE BUSINESS

* OWNERS SKILLS, BACKGROUND, TRAINING

* PRODUCTS OFFERED...full descriptions

* SERVICES OFFERED...benefits, value, etc.

* OVER-HEAD EXPENSES   * OPERATIONAL COSTS

* ANALYSIS OF EXPENSES, COSTS, PROFITS, etc.

* MARKETING PLANS...promotions, coupons, incentives, etc.

* ADVERTISING TECHNIQUES... news, TV, radio, etc.

* PROFIT PRODUCING ASPECTS OF THE BUSINESS

* INCOME PROJECTIONS (monthly, yearly, etc.)

TORNADO TERROR

The need for disaster preparedness critical across America

Tips for Surviving **WEATHER DISASTERS:**

IN THESE TIMES OF EXTREME WEATHER EVENTS --- monster tornadoes, hurricanes, floods, wild-fires and worse – it helps reduce stress for us to know ways of increasing our chances of survival. Follow the instructions given on TV and radio by your city officials, FEMA and others authorized to inform you of potential evacuations and locations of shelters.   In a last-minute evacuation, you don't have time to think, you just want to get out. So be prepared to pick up and move !

Weathering the Storm

Since 2004, more than one billion people around the world have lost their homes, businesses, family members or lives to natural disasters. Proactive preparedness and a clearheaded response will help reduce the stress, mitigate the negative effects...and increase your family's chances of survival.

FLOODS….WILDFIRES…HURRICANES…EARTHQUAKES…

Many people have been saved from injury and death by following a
few simple safety rules —

TORNADO SAFETY RULES:

1. Seek shelter under a sturdy table in the basement. Cover yourself with a large pallet or mattress.

2. If no basement is available, go to a first floor, small interior room, or get into a bathroom on the opposite side from a tornado. Stay away from windows.

3. In schools, churches, and shopping centers, go to designated shelters away from outside walls, glass, and large rooms (malls, auditoriums). Get under a table or counter or in a restroom or small room. **DO NOT GO GET IN A PARKED CAR.**

4. In motels, lie down in the lowest-level interior hallway away from glass. Dive under a bed or pull a mattress on top of you as last resort.

   Go to the lowest point in the house. The basement is best. If you don't have a basement, get into a small closet.

   Evacuate mobile homes, vehicles, boats (and similar) immediately. If you're outside, try and find a shelter – or as a last resort outside --- find a ditch and dive in.

EARTHQUAKE SURVIVAL TIPS:

- **DROP to the ground;** take COVER by getting under a sturdy table or other piece of furniture; and HOLD ON until the shaking stops. If there isn't a table or desk near you, cover your face and head with your arms and crouch in an inside corner of the building.
- **Stay away from glass windows,** outside doors and walls, and anything that could fall, such as lighting fixtures or furniture.
- **Stay in bed if you are there** when the earthquake strikes. Hold on and protect your head with a pillow, unless you are under a heavy light fixture, window or anything else that could fall. In that case, move to the nearest safe place (i.e. under a desk or in an inside corner).
- **Use a doorway for shelter** only if it is in close proximity to you and if you know it is a strongly supported, load-bearing doorway. Brace yourself on the side with the hinges to avoid the door swinging at you.
- **Stay inside until shaking stops** and it is safe to go outside. Research has shown that most injuries occur when people inside buildings attempt to move to a different location inside or try to leave.

Hurricane Risk Reduction

Hurricanes strike suddenly, violently and sometimes without adequate warning. Identifying potential hazards ahead of time and advance planning can reduce the dangers of serious injury or loss of life from a hurricane. Repairing deep plaster cracks in ceilings and foundations, anchoring overhead lighting. To prepare for a hurricane, you should take the following measures--

- Make plans to secure your property. Install shutters or board up windows with plywood. Tape does not prevent windows from breaking.
- Securely fasten your roof to the frame structure.
- Be sure trees and shrubs around your home are well trimmed.
- Determine how and where to secure your vehicles and boat.
- If you can afford it -- consider building a 'safe room' or other shelter.
- **Draft an evacuation plan,** map out your way toward safety and shelter.

DISASTER SURVIVAL KIT

Prepare or purchase a **"Survival Kit"** – that contains some basic items that you will need **just in case** the power goes out – banks and stores are closed, you get stranded in a damaged house, and/or ------- perhaps...*if* **FEMA** *takes too long to show up.*

FOR MORE INFO ON DISASTER SURVIVAL -- **www.redcross.org**

STOCK UP IN ADVANCE -- Use a large water proof

(plastic) containers – and bags to store your **"Survival Kit"** and keep it where you can easily find it and get to the items. You should find water-proof bags in which you keep important documents – *such as:* ID CARDS, BIRTH CERTIFICATES, ID CARDS, BANKING RECORDS, DEEDS, TITLES, INSURANCE POLICIES, MEDICAL RECORDS, KEEPSAKE PHOTOS, DEGREES, AWARDS, CASH…and anything else that is important or that you consider valuable and *"hard to replace."*

Make sure you have the basic items in a plastic case, duffel bags, and other packaging that is portable -- that you would need in case you are stranded in your house – and have no access to electricity, heat, clean water, food, washers, banks, or medical assistance.

BASIC ITEMS FOR YOUR SURVIVAL KIT –

- **Water bottles** – Drinking Water- (and tablets for purifying) – at least a one week supply for each person. Most experts recommend a gallon of water, per person for each day.

- **NO LESS THAN A 3-DAY SUPPLY OF FOOD**….but it would be better to have 7 to 14 days of Non-Perishable Foods- such as: Instant oatmeal, canned meat or fish, -- also: cereals, peanut butter, juices, instant food mixes, nutritional energy bars, granola, trail mix, instant rice, tea.

- **CAMPING SUPPLIES** -- Disposable plates, cups, pots, and spoons, forks, utensils ….manual can and bottle opener…blankets, raincoats, etc.

- **Extra batteries**…. and Battery-operated radio or weather radio.

- **Solar-powered or camping lantern** – pick one that runs on an extended battery. Also include matches and candles.

- **FIRST AID KIT**….Pick one with pain relievers, aspirin, eye wash, bandages, cotton, antacids, diarrhea medication, anti-biotic creams.

- **Personal care items**- toothbrushes, toothpaste, hair brush, soap, shampoo, towels, feminine products, toilet and tissue paper. At least one change of clothes for each family member, light jackets, boots, hats, shoes and socks.

- **TOOLS** – hammer, ax, wrench, screwdrivers, small shovel, and any others that might be easily stored.

- **SUPPLIES FOR PETS** -- if you have a pet – be sure to include food, medicines, and supplies for pets – and any important records.

Think like the Scouts --- **BE PREPARED !**

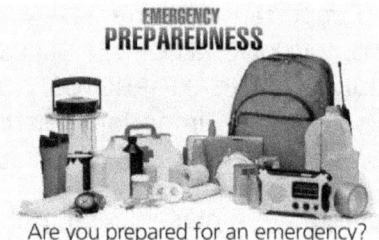

Build your own *Eco-Survival Kit*

...contains: flash lights, batteries, water bottles, candles, matches, masks, can opener, duct tape, tools, moist towelettes, first aid supplies, energy bars, freeze-dried/canned foods & drinks, rubber gloves, tissue, health products, DVD, edutainment books *& more !...*

A **MUST-HAVE** FOR HOME OR OFFICE IN THESE UNCERTAIN TIMES OF DISASTERS.

YOU COULD WIN A FREE HOLISTIC **FIRST AID KIT:**

EDUTAINMENT EXERCISES and ACTIVITIES

"A wise teacher makes learning enjoyable...."

Created by Author Melvia Miller, who specializes in *"Edu-tainment"*

Author **Melvia Miller** has designed games and activities that enhance the learning process. She developed books and games for teens and adults. Educational Research shows that classes are most effective when we utilize our senses, minds, hands, and are involved in activities. No amount of lecturing can bring about the wonderous outcomes that are derived from these types of interactive games and activities.

ROCK SCHOOL GAME

GOALS & OBJECTIVES

To practice answering questions with facts...and to learn more about history, ecology, health, or other subjects.

MATERIALS NEEDED:

* This game is best played on a set of steps or bleachers. Each step is considered to be a "grade level"--- e.g. *"First grade, second grade, third grade,* etc."
     The **top step** is GRADUATION.

* Prepare a list of at least 100 questions with their answers---on the facts and events   of Black History.

EXAMPLE:
*Q= **What is the name of the famous Black Basketball team that began in 1927 and won more than 8,000 games?**

* Answer = **The Harlem Globetrotters.**

HOW TO PLAY THIS GAME:

    The group leader or teacher hides a small stone or rock in one hand, with both hands behind his/her back....as s/he faces the players who are sitting on the steps.   Each player will take a turn to guess which hand the teacher is hiding the stone. If the player guesses correctly, then the teacher gives this same player one of the QUESTIONS to answer. If the player answers correctly, s/he gets to move up one step.   Then the next player gets a turn to do the same.   Each player will have no more than one minute to give their answer to each question.
    If the player does not get the right answer as to which hand the rock is in...the player loses his/her turn. If the player does not get the correct answer to the question, the player has gets demoted one step (and must move down one step). Players move up & down the steps until someone reaches the top.

THE WINNER is the player who reaches the top step first.
* Prizes can be awarded to the players who reach the top grades.

'SAVE THE PLANET' Activity

SUPPLIES = A spinner or dice and white board or small easel.

INSTRUCTIONS = * Players divide into teams of 2 people. Each player than take turns spinning the wheel. Whatever number comes up...player must explain that number of ways that we can **"help save the planet"** -- such as: *increasing recycling, planting trees, saving rainforests, using natural health remedies, etc.*

For example...if player spins **3** on the wheel – then both players on that team must make a simple sketch of **3 valid ideas** for that it would be good for *ECOLOGY*.

*Then player must give a reason that his/her selected *"natural remedies"* can be beneficial.   *FOR EXAMPLE.....*

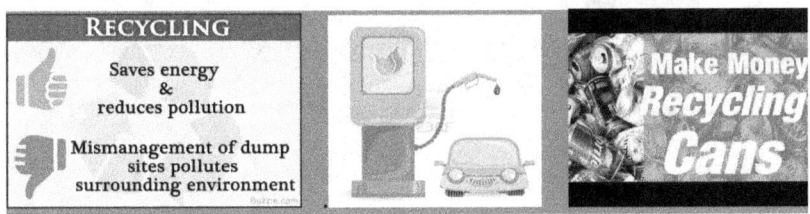

Non-*polluting fuels can be made from* **Hemp** *and* **Algae oil** *cheaper than it costs to drill for crude oil.*

EACH TEAM WILL THEN SELECT THEIR BEST RESPONSE AND PREPARE

A SIMPLE SKETCH TO PRESENT TO THE GROUP OR CLASS.

SKETCHES CAN BE TURNED INTO POSTERS FOR SPECIAL EVENTS, *such as:* *"Earth Day Displays"* ...or *"Natural Health Fair Expo"*
Or...TEACHER CAN ASSESS WHICH SKETCHES SHOW THE MOST CREATIVE and/or BENEFICIAL IDEAS FOR SAVING THE PLANET.

WHO WANTS TO BE A MILLIONAIRE?

Objectives: To help participants learn the language of business, money, and success--- and to be able to define what is needed to succeed in business.

This game is then played just like the one on TV, except to make it more fun, 2 contestants (participants) will play (compete) against each other.

Supplies needed:
- Timer
- Tablet
- 3" X 5" cards
- Play money (such as used in Monopoly)
- Poster Board and marker

Preparation---

On poster board, prepare a chart that shows the amount of money that will be awarded for each correct answer. The amounts should progressively move up to one million dollars.

Before starting the game, participants must prepare a list of at least 100 "business words & concepts" on a sheet of paper. Use concepts such as: goal setting, corporation, Board of Directors, marketing, advertising, cash flow, tax deductions, etc.

Then, the group will turn these concepts into "multiple choice" questions. Each one should be typed onto a card, thus preparing a deck of these questions for use in the game.

FOR EXAMPLE:

What is a corporation?
- a) A type of training program
- b) The name of a military operation in Asia
- c) A legal form of business
- d) A foreign food made with rice

One person will serve as the facilitator and will be the "caller" who pulls a card out of the deck which has one of the multiple choice problems on it. Players will take turns competing for each level of money. The 2 competing participants will have one minute to give the correct answer to each question. Wrong answers get zero money. If at any time one of the players misses 3 questions ---they are out. Another player is then selected to play against the winner.

Correct answers will be awarded the money that is listed on the chart.

THE ULTIMATE WINNER...is the player who beats all the other players or who wins the MILLION DOLLARS.

WHAT PEOPLE ARE SAYING -

" Melvia Miller is remarkable. She has the vision--the dream of racial harmony and peace on Earth. To write about this topic with laughter and love is brilliant." --

~from Ms. **Dottie Walters**, author of *"SPEAK & GROW RICH"*

****

"Melvia Miller brings to her work a solid background as an educator and a member of a minority group, which make her books of a true multi-cultural perspective. "

...~from **Dr. Penny Ralston**, Dean -- Florida State Univ.

****

**"I am indeed impressed with Melvia's books.
I look forward to reading more from her."**

~ from Dr. **Gloria Murray,** Professor -- Indiana Univ. --Louisville

****

"Melvia's books are very useful, excellent, and inspiring."

~from **Dr. Carmela Corallo Jackson,**
*(Director of Infinite Winds Counseling Center--- of Encinitas, CA)

****

"Melvia Miller writes an excellent brand of poetry." -

~by **Max Robinson**, (ABC-TV news anchorman)

"I have known this author for many years – and she always could tell a good story. I really enjoy reading these books by Melvia Miller because she is so informative and hits the nail on the head as to what the problem is and ways to solve it. Her books cover complicated topics, but simple to understand."

~ **Ms. V. Richardson**, Retired Nurse (Indiana)

ABOUT THE AUTHOR

Author **Melvia Miller** is an advocate for new and innovative ways of teaching and learning, such as using games, exercises, creative, critical thinking activities, and group processes --- for *"wholistic eco-education"* that helps increase our awareness and empower people to achieve. She is the creator of board games and also the author of several books, including:

- *Eco-Health*
- *New and Different Friends*
- *Sickos, Psychos and Stormy Weather*
- *Think Outside*

An award-winning educator/author, she has taught in the public schools and in universities and colleges. Melvia F. Miller is an expert in the area of designing educational 'multi-cultural' materials for teaching 'Cultural Diversity,' Black History & Environmental Studies.

She has received many honors and awards, fellowships, and scholarships, including having been named to *"Who's Who in American Universities & Colleges."* and to *"Who's Who in America."* She has received many other honors, including being named: *"Young Professional Woman of the Year"*--by NANBPW, Inc. ---and she is a graduate of the University of Michigan and Ball State University. Melvia holds several advanced degrees in Multi-Cultural Education, Instructional Design, and ECO- Psychology Education. She is also a member of *Delta Sigma Theta Public Sorority.*

And she is the mother of 2 sons: **Malik** & **Mikal**

Melvia is also the author of several other books, manuals & DVDs.

* www.authorsden.com/melviafmiller